AF201090

Impressum
Verlag: BABADADA GmbH, Nedderfeld 112 , 22529 Hamburg
Geschäftsführer / Verlagsleitung: Harald Hof
Druck: Books on Demand GmbH, In de Tarpen 42, 22848 Norderstedt

Imprint
Publisher: BABADADA GmbH, Nedderfeld 112 , 22529 Hamburg, Germany
Managing Director / Publishing direction: Harald Hof
Print: Books on Demand GmbH, In de Tarpen 42, 22848 Norderstedt

school
Schule

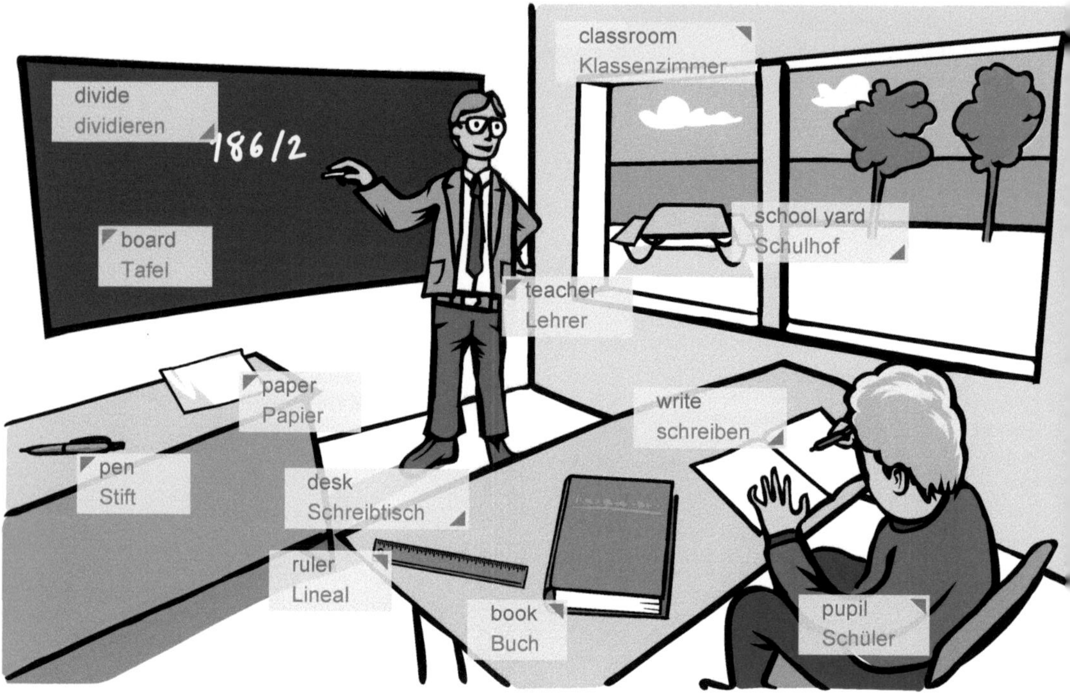
classroom
Klassenzimmer
divide
dividieren
186/2
board
Tafel
school yard
Schulhof
teacher
Lehrer
paper
Papier
write
schreiben
pen
Stift
desk
Schreibtisch
ruler
Lineal
book
Buch
pupil
Schüler

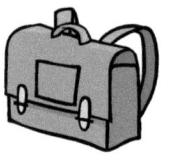

satchel

Schultasche

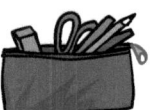

pencil case

Federmappe

pencil

Bleistift

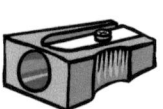

pencil sharpener

Bleistiftspitzer

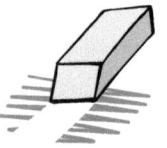

rubber

Radierer

drawing pad

Zeichenblock

drawing

Zeichnung

paintbrush

Pinsel

paint box

Malkasten

scissors

Schere

glue

Klebstoff

exercise book

Übungsheft

homework

Hausübung

number

Zahl

add

addieren

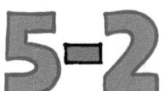

subtract

subtrahieren

multiply

multiplizieren

calculate

rechnen

letter

Buchstabe

alphabet

Alphabet

word

Wort

text
Text

read
lesen

chalk
Kreide

lesson
Unterrichtsstunde

register
Klassenbuch

examination
Prüfung

certificate
Zeugnis

school uniform
Schuluniform

education
Ausbildung

encyclopedia
Lexikon

university
Universität

microscope
Mikroskop

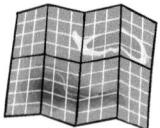

map
Karte

waste-paper basket
Papierkorb

travel
Reise

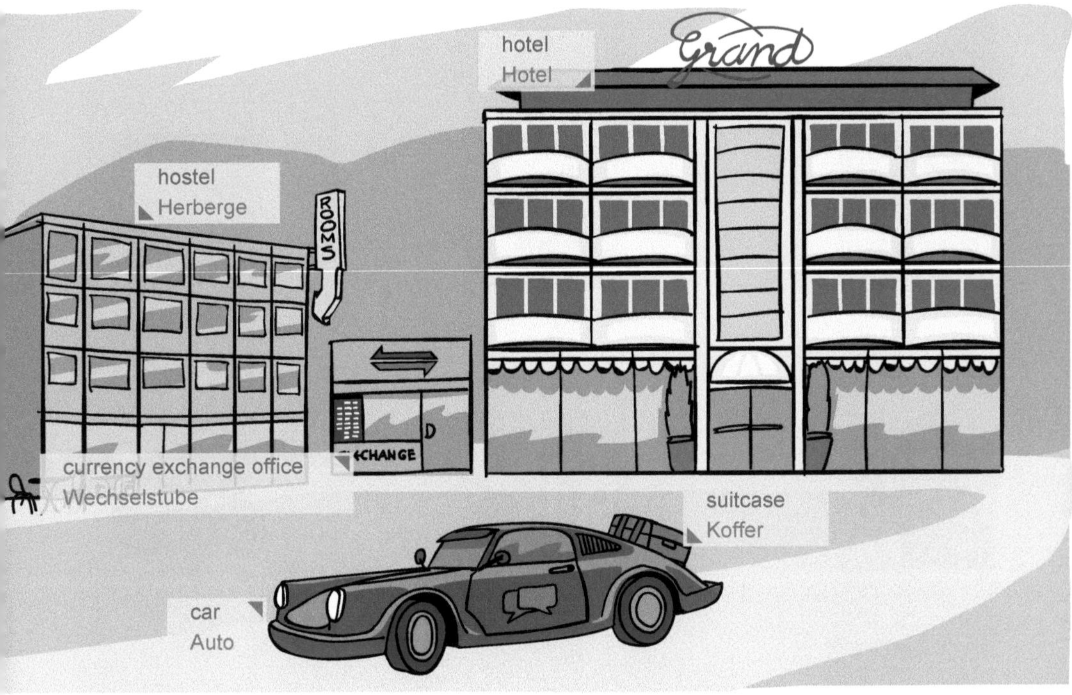
hotel
Hotel
Grand
hostel
Herberge
ROOMS
currency exchange office
Wechselstube
EXCHANGE
suitcase
Koffer
car
Auto

language
Sprache

yes / no
ja / nein

Okay
Okay

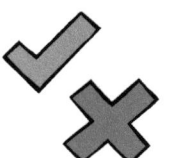

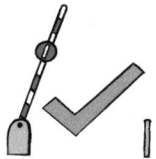

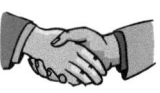

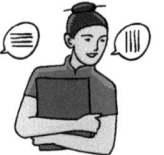

hello
Hallo

translator
Dolmetscherin

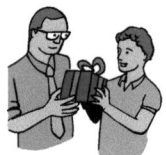

Thank you
Danke

how much is…?

Wie viel kostet …?

I don't get it

Ich verstehe nicht.

problem

Problem

Good evening!

Guten Abend!

Good morning!

Guten Morgen!

Good night!

Gute Nacht!

goodbye

Auf Wiederschaun!

direction

Richtung

luggage

Gepäck

bag

Tasche

backpack

Rucksack

guest

Gast

room

Zimmer

sleeping bag

Schlafsack

tent

Zelt

travel - Reise

tourist information

Touristeninformation

beach

Strand

credit card

Kreditkarte

breakfast

Frühstück

lunch

Mittagessen

dinner

Abendessen

Ticket

Fahrkarte

elevator

Lift

stamp

Briefmarke

border

Grenze

customs

Zoll

embassy

Botschaft

visa

Visum

passport

Pass

transport
Transport

airplane
Flugzeug

ship
Schiff

fire truck
Feuerwehrauto

bus
Bus

truck
Lastwagen

motorboat
Motorboot

bike
Fahrrad

car
Auto

ferry

Fähre

boat

Boot

motorbike

Motorrad

police car

Polizeiauto

racing car

Rennauto

rental car

Mietwagen

car sharing

Carsharing

tow truck

Abschleppwagen

garbage truck

Müllwagen

engine

Motor

fuel

Kraftstoff

fuel station

Tankstelle

traffic sign

Verkehrsschild

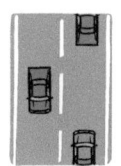

traffic

Verkehr

traffic jam

Stau

parking lot

Parkplatz

train station

Bahnhof

tracks

Schienen

train

Zug

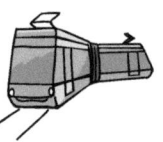

tram

Straßenbahn

wagon

Wagon

helicopter

Hubschrauber

airport

Flughafen

tower

Tower

passenger

Passagier

container

Container

carton

Karton

cart

Rollwagen

basket

Korb

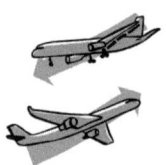

take off / land

starten / landen

city

Stadt

village

Dorf

city center

Stadtzentrum

house

Haus

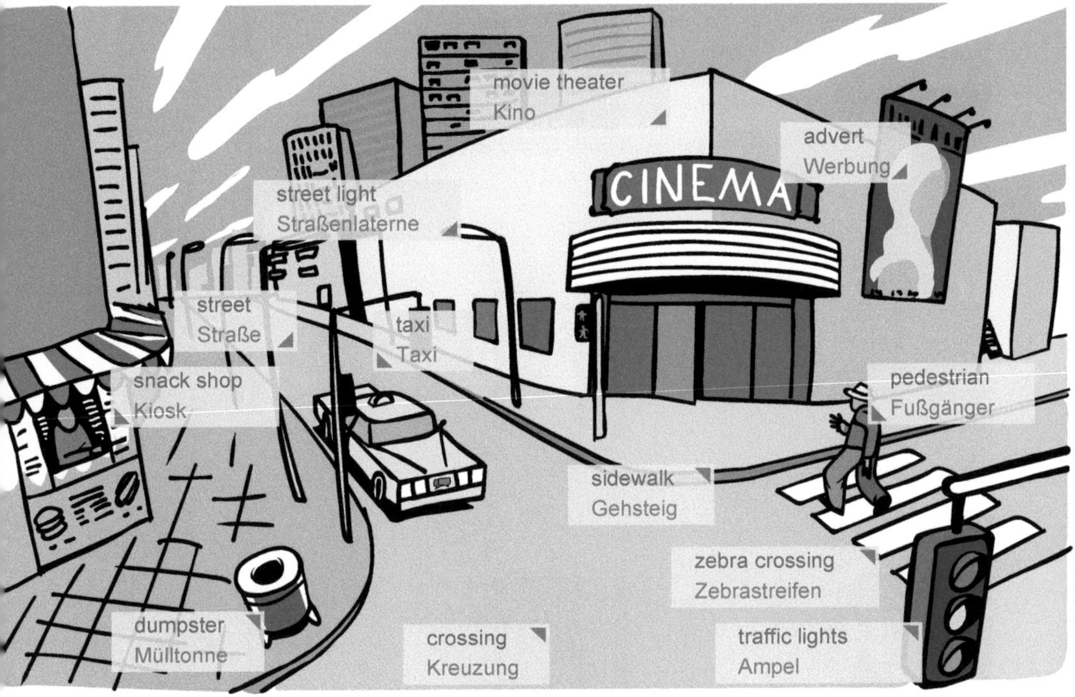

movie theater
Kino

advert
Werbung

street light
Straßenlaterne

CINEMA

street
Straße

taxi
Taxi

snack shop
Kiosk

pedestrian
Fußgänger

sidewalk
Gehsteig

zebra crossing
Zebrastreifen

dumpster
Mülltonne

crossing
Kreuzung

traffic lights
Ampel

hut

Hütte

apartment

Wohnung

train station

Bahnhof

city hall

Rathaus

museum

Museum

school

Schule

city - Stadt

university

Universität

bank

Bank

hospital

Spital

hotel

Hotel

pharmacy

Apotheke

office

Büro

book shop

Buchhandlung

shop

Geschäft

flower shop

Blumenladen

supermarket

Supermarkt

market

Markt

department store

Kaufhaus

fishmonger's shop

Fischhändler

mall

Einkaufszentrum

harbor

Hafen

park

Park

bench

Bank

bridge

Brücke

stairs

Stiege

subway

U-Bahn

tunnel

Tunnel

bus stop

Bushaltestelle

bar

Bar

restaurant

Restaurant

postbox

Briefkasten

street sign

Straßenschild

parking meter

Parkuhr

zoo

Zoo

swimming pool

Badeanstalt

mosque

Moschee

farm
Bauernhof

pollution
Umweltverschmutzung

cemetery
Friedhof

church
Kirche

playground
Spielplatz

temple
Tempel

landscape
Landschaft

leaf
Blatt

signpost
Wegweiser

path
Weg

meadow
Wiese

stone
Stein

tree
Baum

hiker
Wanderer

river
Fluss

grass
Gras

flower
Blume

valley

Tal

hill

Hügel

lake

See

forest

Wald

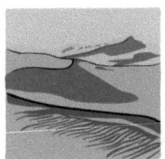

desert

Wüste

volcano

Vulkan

castle

Schloss

rainbow

Regenbogen

mushroom

Pilz

palm tree

Palme

mosquito

Moskito

fly

Fliege

ant

Ameise

bee

Biene

spider

Spinne

beetle

Käfer

frog

Frosch

squirrel

Eichhörnchen

hedgehog

Igel

hare

Hase

owl

Eule

bird

Vogel

swan

Schwan

boar

Wildschwein

deer

Hirsch

moose

Elch

dam

Staudamm

wind turbine

Windrad

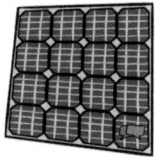

solar panel

Solarmodul

climate

Klima

restaurant
Restaurant

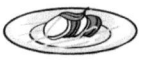

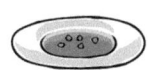

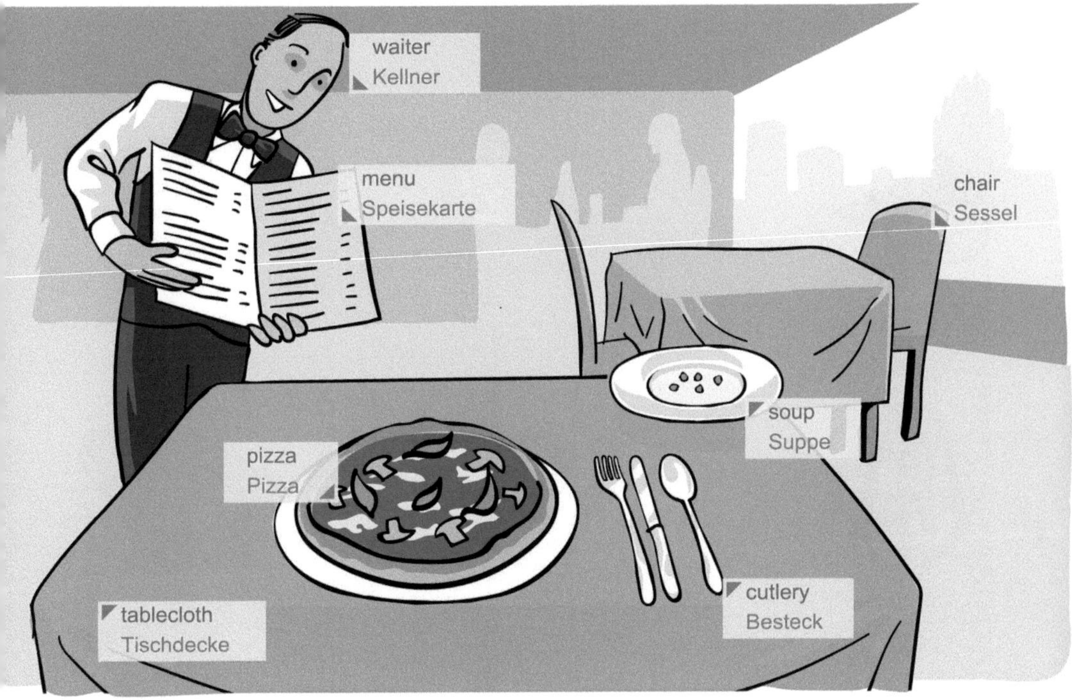
waiter
Kellner
menu
Speisekarte
chair
Sessel
soup
Suppe
pizza
Pizza
cutlery
Besteck
tablecloth
Tischdecke

starter

Vorspeise

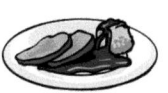

main course

Hauptgericht

dessert

Nachspeise

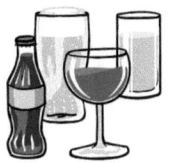

drinks

Getränke

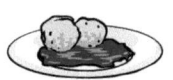

food

Essen

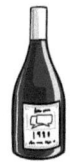

bottle

Flasche

fast food

Fastfood

street food

Streetfood

teapot

Teekanne

sugar bowl

Zuckerdose

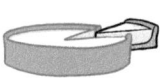

portion

Portion

espresso machine

Espressomaschine

high chair

Kinderstuhl

bill

Rechnung

tray

Tablett

knife

Messer

fork

Gabel

spoon

Löffel

teaspoon

Teelöffel

serviette

Serviette

glass

Glas

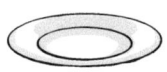

plate

Teller

soup plate

Suppenteller

saucer

Untertasse

sauce

Sauce

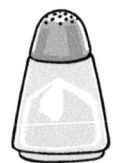

salt shaker

Salzstreuer

pepper mill

Pfeffermühle

vinegar

Essig

oil

Öl

spices

Gewürze

ketchup

Ketchup

mustard

Senf

mayonnaise

Mayonnaise

supermarket
Supermarkt

special offer
Angebot
FOR
customer
Kunde
dairy products
Milchprodukte
fruit
Obst
shopping cart
Einkaufswagen

BUTCHERS

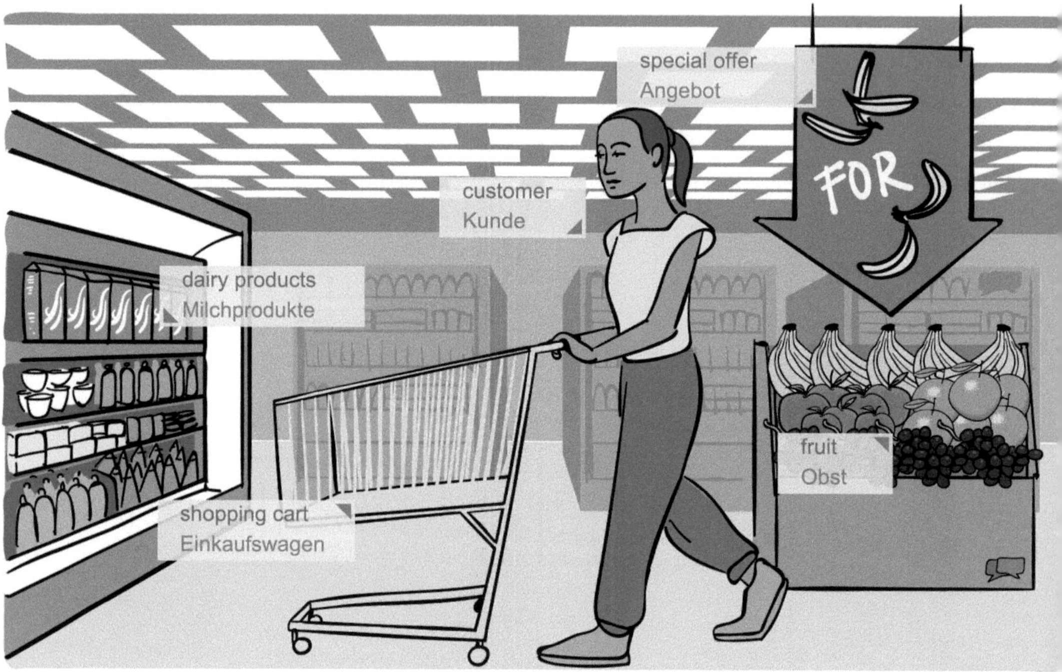

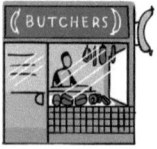

butcher's shop

Schlachterei

BAKERY

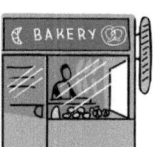

bakery

Bäckerei

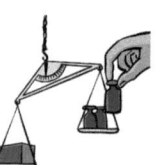

weigh

wiegen

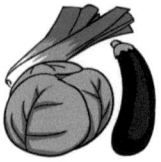

vegetables

Gemüse

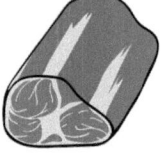

meat

Fleisch

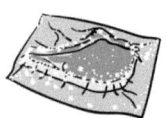

frozen food

Tiefkühlkost

cold cuts

Aufschnitt

canned food

Konserven

detergent

Waschmittel

candy

Süßigkeiten

household products

Haushaltsartikel

cleaning products

Reinigungsmittel

sales representative

Verkäuferin

cash register

Kassa

cashier

Kassiererin

shopping list

Einkaufsliste

opening hours

Öffnungszeiten

wallet

Brieftasche

credit card

Kreditkarte

bag

Tasche

plastic bag

Plastiktüte

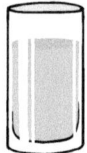

water

Wasser

juice

Saft

milk

Milch

coke

Cola

wine

Wein

beer

Bier

alcohol

Alkohol

cocoa

Kakao

tea

Tee

coffee

Kaffee

espresso

Espresso

cappuccino

Cappuccino

banana

Banane

apple

Apfel

orange

Orange

melon

Melone

lemon

Zitrone

carrot

Karotte

garlic

Knoblauch

bamboo

Bambus

onion

Zwiebel

mushroom

Pilz

nuts

Nüsse

noodles

Nudeln

spaghetti

Spaghetti

rice

Reis

salad

Salat

fries

Pommes frites

fried potatoes

Bratkartoffeln

pizza

Pizza

hamburger

Hamburger

sandwich

Sandwich

escalope

Schnitzel

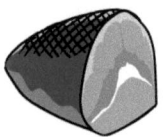

ham

Schinken

salami

Salami

sausage

Wurst

chicken

Huhn

roast

Braten

fish

Fisch

porridge oats

Haferflocken

muesli

Müsli

cornflakes

Cornflakes

flour

Mehl

croissant

Croissant

bread roll

Semmel

bread

Brot

toast

Toast

cookies

Kekse

butter

Butter

curd

Topfen

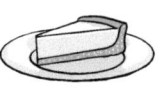

cake

Kuchen

egg

Ei

fried egg

Spiegelei

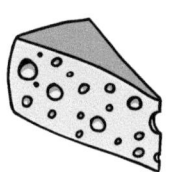

cheese

Käse

ice cream

Eiscreme

sugar

Zucker

honey

Honig

jelly

Marmelade

nougat cream

Schokoladenaufstrich

curry

Curry

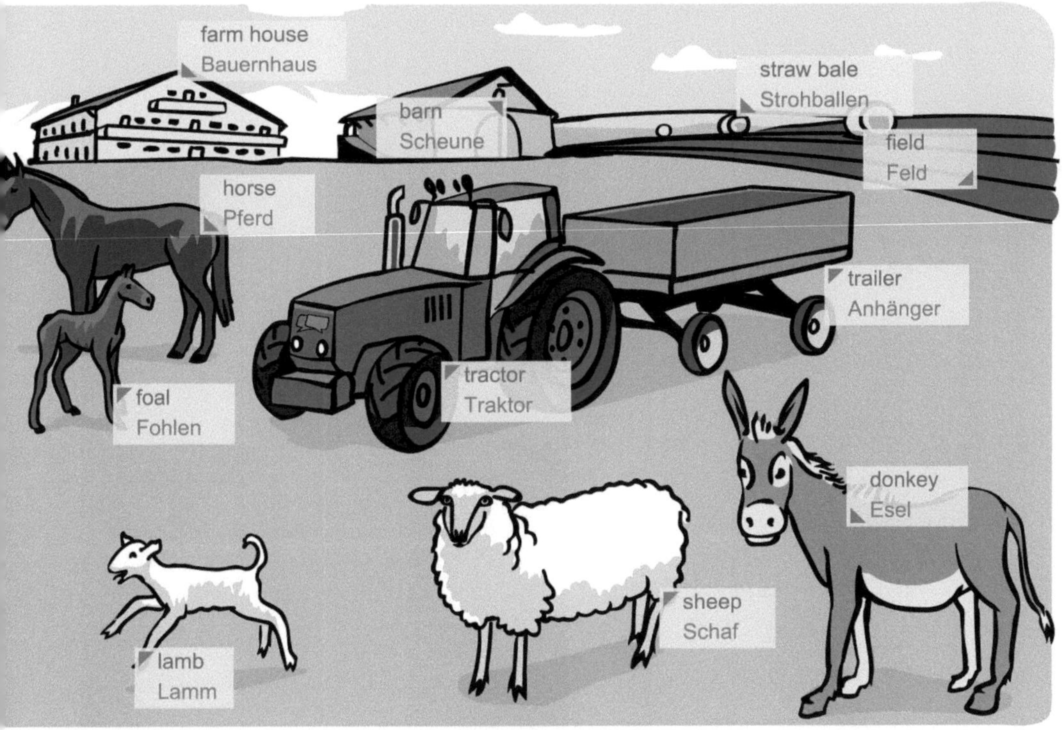

farm house
Bauernhaus

straw bale
Strohballen

barn
Scheune

field
Feld

horse
Pferd

trailer
Anhänger

foal
Fohlen

tractor
Traktor

donkey
Esel

lamb
Lamm

sheep
Schaf

goat
Ziege

cow
Kuh

calf
Kalb

pig
Schwein

piglet
Ferkel

bull
Stier

goose

Gans

duck

Ente

chick

Küken

hen

Huhn

cockerel

Hahn

rat

Ratte

cat

Katze

mouse

Maus

ox

Ochse

dog

Hund

dog house

Hundehütte

garden hose

Gartenschlauch

watering can

Gießkanne

scythe

Sense

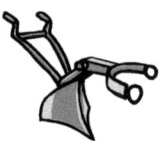

plow

Pflug

sickle

Sichel

hoe

Hacke

pitchfork

Mistgabel

axe

Axt

pushcart

Schubkarre

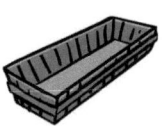

trough

Trog

milk can

Milchkanne

sack

Sack

fence

Zaun

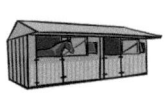

stable

Stall

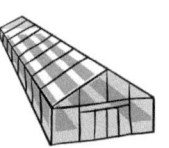

greenhouse

Treibhaus

soil

Boden

seed

Saat

fertilizer

Dünger

combine harvester

Mähdrescher

harvest

ernten

harvest

Ernte

yams

Yamswurzel

wheat

Weizen

soya

Soja

potato

Erdapfel

corn

Mais

rapeseed

Raps

fruit tree

Obstbaum

manioc

Maniok

grain

Getreide

house

Haus

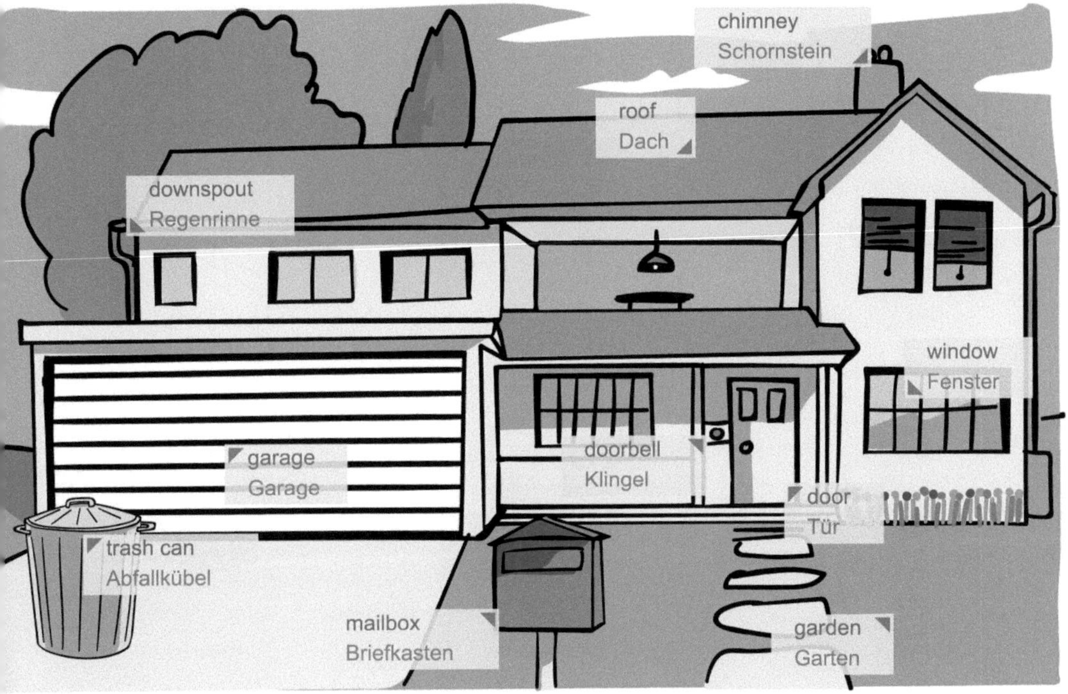
chimney
Schornstein
roof
Dach
downspout
Regenrinne
window
Fenster
doorbell
Klingel
garage
Garage
door
Tür
trash can
Abfallkübel
mailbox
Briefkasten
garden
Garten

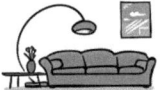

living room

Wohnzimmer

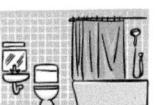

bathroom

Badezimmer

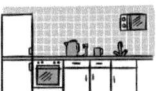

kitchen

Küche

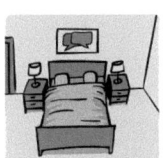

bedroom

Schlafzimmer

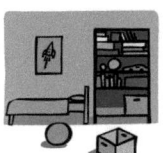

kids room

Kinderzimmer

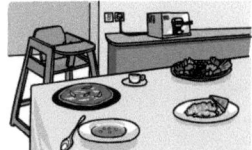

dining room

Esszimmer

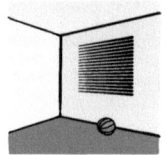

floor

Boden

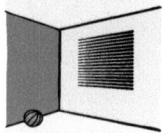

wall

Wand

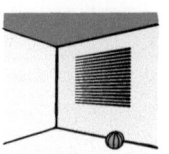

ceiling

Decke

cellar

Keller

sauna

Sauna

balcony

Balkon

terrace

Terrasse

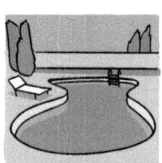

pool

Schwimmbad

lawn mower

Rasenmäher

sheet

Bettbezug

bedspread

Bettdecke

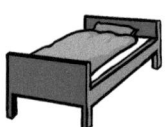

bed

Bett

broom

Besen

bucket

Kübel

switch

Schalter

living room

Wohnzimmer

wallpaper
Tapete
picture
Bild
lamp
Lampe
shelf
Regal
cabinet
Schrank
television
Fernseher
fireplace
Kamin
flower
Blume
cushion
Polster
sofa
Sofa
vase
Vase
remote control
Fernbedienung

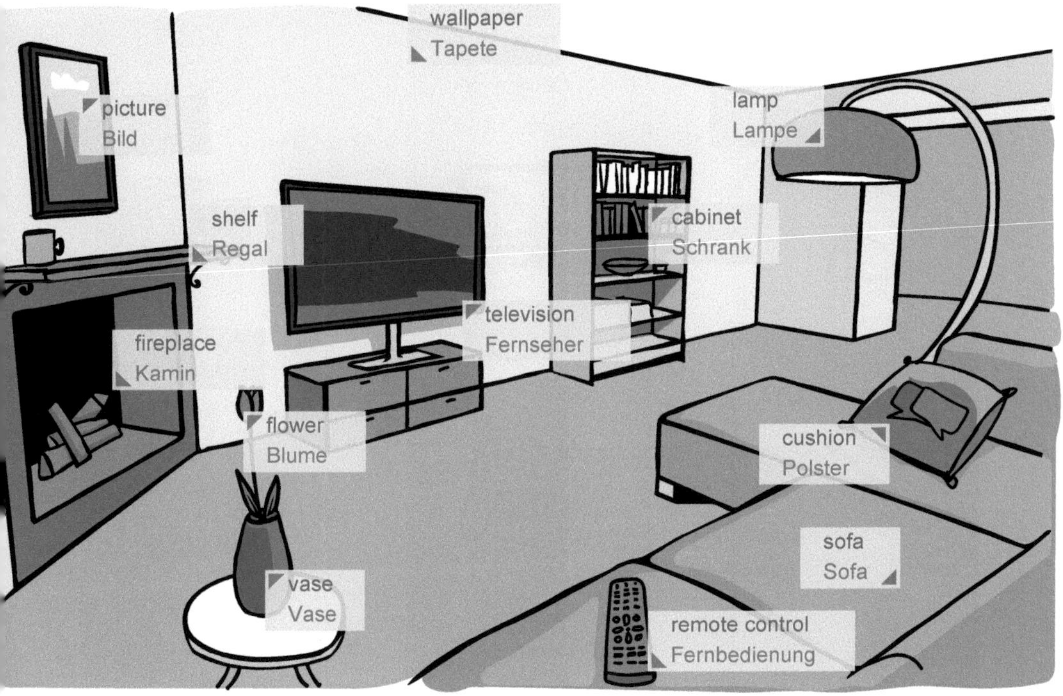

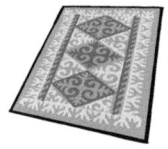

carpet

Teppich

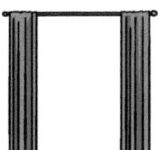

drape

Vorhang

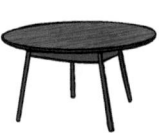

table

Tisch

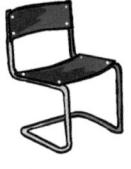

chair

Sessel

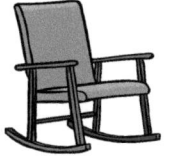

rocking chair

Schaukelstuhl

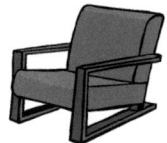

armchair

Sessel

book

Buch

blanket

Decke

decoration

Dekoration

firewood

Feuerholz

film

Film

stereo system

Stereoanlage

key

Schlüssel

newspaper

Zeitung

painting

Gemälde

poster

Poster

radio

Radio

notebook

Notizblock

vacuum cleaner

Staubsauger

cactus

Kaktus

candle

Kerze

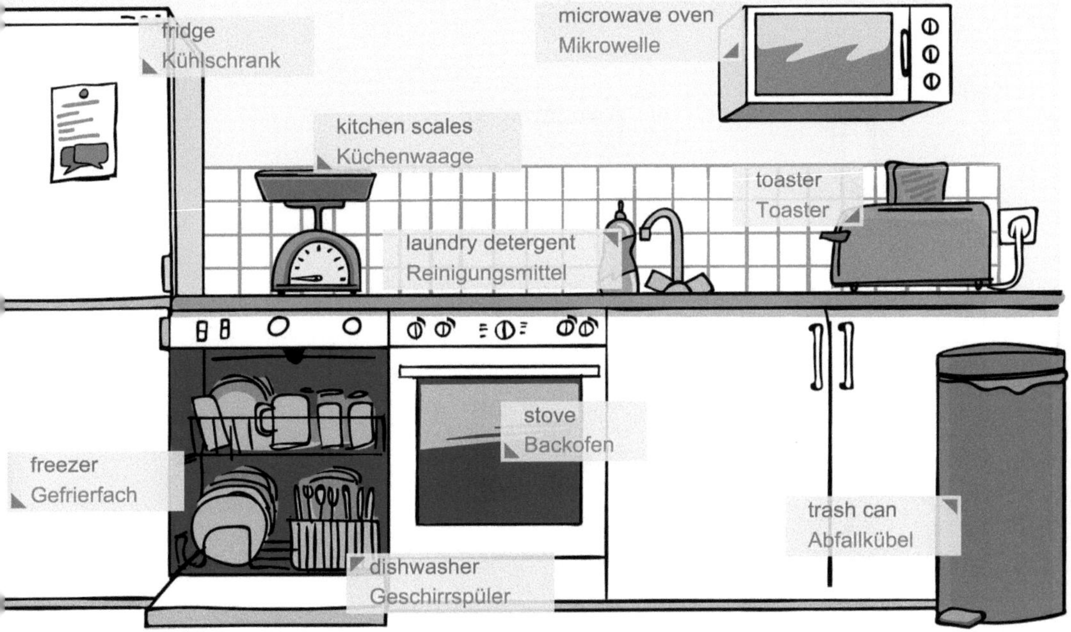

fridge
Kühlschrank

microwave oven
Mikrowelle

kitchen scales
Küchenwaage

toaster
Toaster

laundry detergent
Reinigungsmittel

stove
Backofen

freezer
Gefrierfach

trash can
Abfallkübel

dishwasher
Geschirrspüler

cooker

Herd

pot

Topf

cast-iron pot

Eisentopf

wok / kadai

Wok / Kadai

pan

Pfanne

kettle

Wasserkocher

steamer

Dampfgarer

baking tray

Backblech

crockery

Geschirr

mug

Becher

bowl

Schale

chopsticks

Essstäbchen

ladle

Schöpflöffel

spatula

Pfannenwender

whisk

Schneebesen

strainer

Kochsieb

sieve

Sieb

grater

Reibe

mortar

Mörser

barbecue

Grill

fireplace

Kaminfeuer

chopping board

Schneidebrett

rolling pin

Nudelholz

corkscrew

Korkenzieher

can

Dose

can opener

Dosenöffner

oven cloth

Topflappen

sink

Waschbecken

brush

Bürste

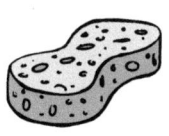

sponge

Schwamm

blender

Mixer

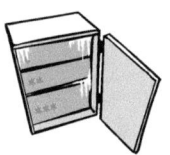

deep freezer

Gefriertruhe

baby bottle

Babyflasche

tap

Wasserhahn

kitchen - Küche

bathroom
Badezimmer

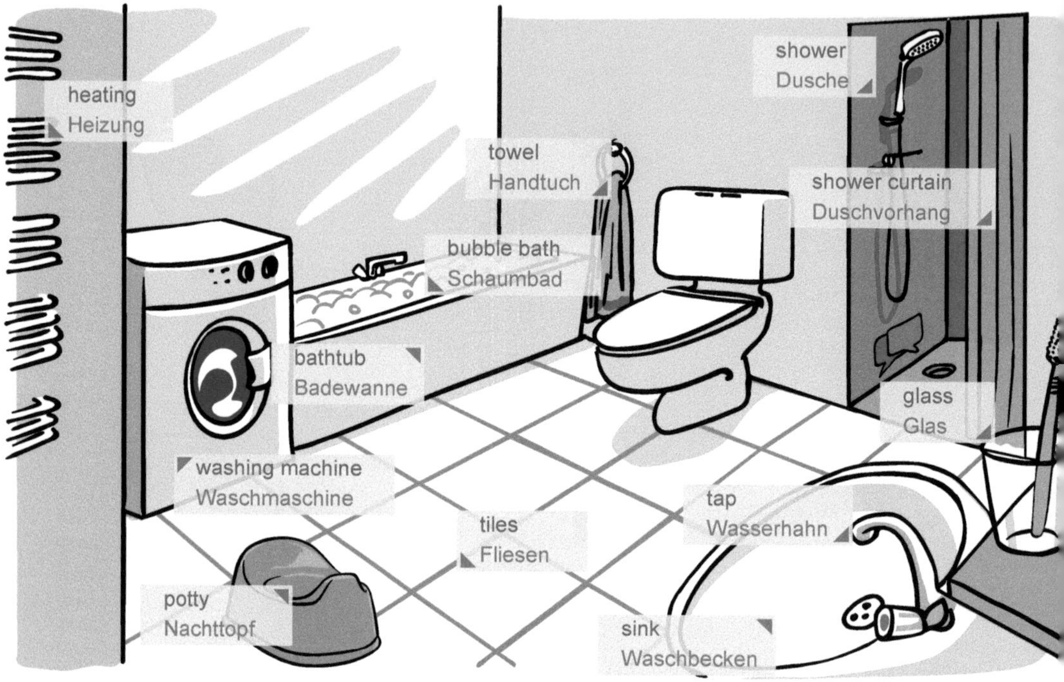

heating
Heizung
shower
Dusche
towel
Handtuch
shower curtain
Duschvorhang
bubble bath
Schaumbad
bathtub
Badewanne
glass
Glas
washing machine
Waschmaschine
tap
Wasserhahn
tiles
Fliesen
potty
Nachttopf
sink
Waschbecken

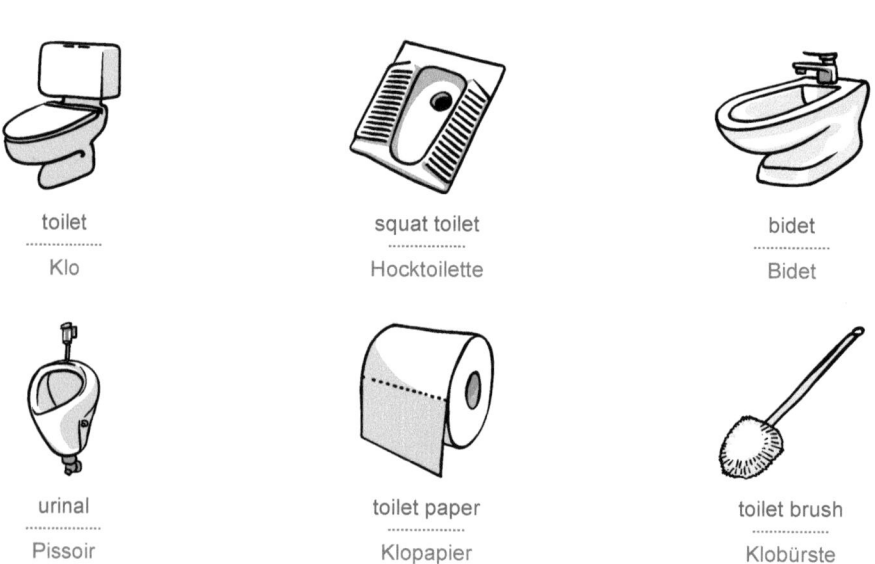

toilet

Klo

squat toilet

Hocktoilette

bidet

Bidet

urinal

Pissoir

toilet paper

Klopapier

toilet brush

Klobürste

toothbrush

Zahnbürste

toothpaste

Zahnpasta

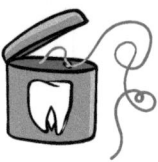

dental floss

Zahnseide

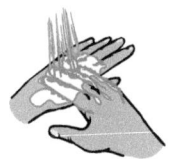

wash

waschen

hand shower

Handbrause

douche

Intimdusche

basin

Waschschüssel

back brush

Rückenbürste

soap

Seife

shower gel

Duschgel

shampoo

Shampoo

flannel

Waschlappen

drain

Abfluss

creme

Creme

deodorant

Deodorant

mirror

Spiegel

hand mirror

Kosmetikspiegel

razor

Rasierer

shaving foam

Rasierschaum

aftershave

Rasierwasser

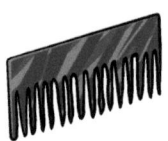

comb

Kamm

brush

Bürste

hair-dryer

Föhn

hairspray

Haarspray

makeup

Makeup

lipstick

Lippenstift

nail varnish

Nagellack

cotton wool

Watte

nail scissors

Nagelschere

perfume

Parfum

washbag

Kulturbeutel

stool

Hocker

weighing scales

Waage

bathrobe

Bademantel

rubber gloves

Gummihandschuhe

tampon

Tampon

sanitary towel

Damenbinde

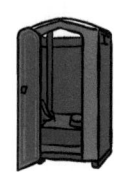

chemical toilet

Chemietoilette

kids room
Kinderzimmer

alarm clock
Wecker
cuddly toy
Kuscheltier
toy car
Spielzeugauto
rattle
Rassel
doll's house
Puppenhaus
present
Geschenk

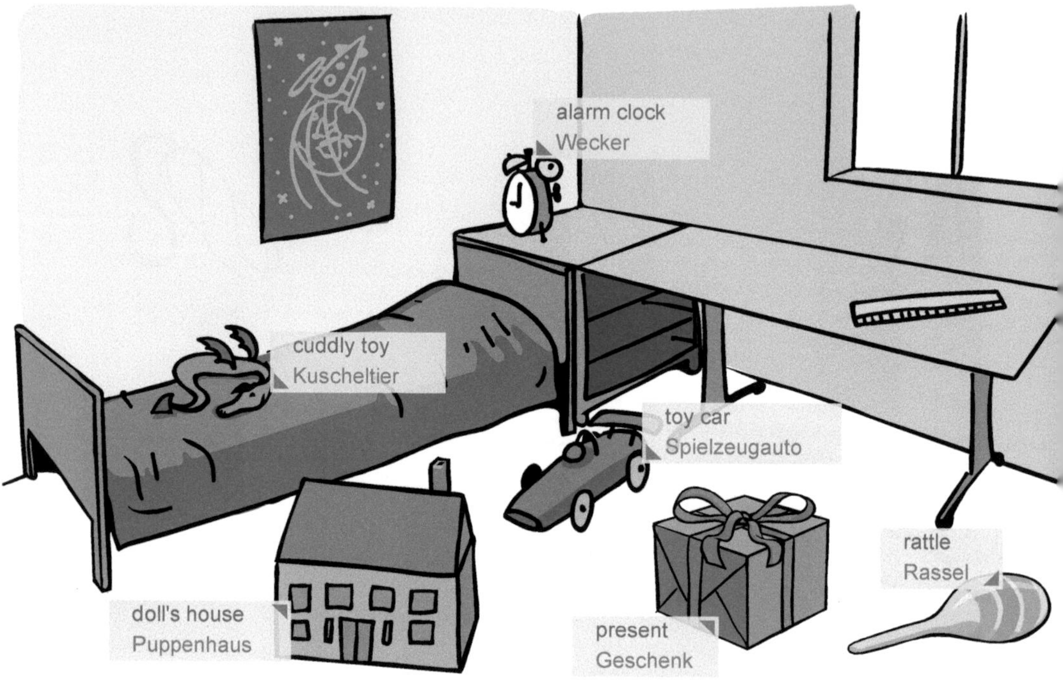

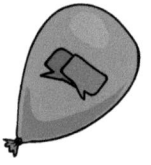

balloon

Ballon

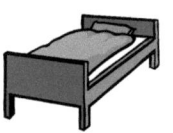

bed

Bett

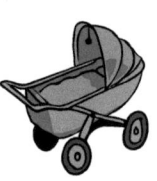

stroller

Kinderwagen

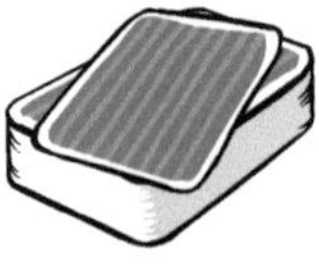

deck of cards

Kartenspiel

jigsaw

Puzzle

SUPER
MEGA

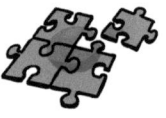

comic

Comic

lego bricks

Legosteine

toy blocks

Bausteine

action figure

Actionfigur

romper suit

Strampelanzug

frisbee

Frisbee

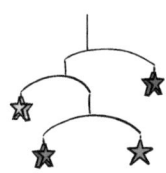

mobile

Mobile

board game

Brettspiel

dice

Würfel

model train set

Modelleisenbahn

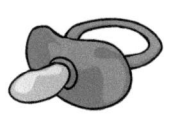

pacifier

Schnuller

party

Party

picture book

Bilderbuch

ball

Ball

doll

Puppe

play

spielen

kids room - Kinderzimmer

sandpit

Sandkasten

swing

Schaukel

toys

Spielzeug

video game console

Spielkonsole

tricycle

Dreirad

teddy bear

Teddy

wardrobe

Kleiderschrank

clothing
Kleidung

socks

Socken

stockings

Strümpfe

tights

Strumpfhose

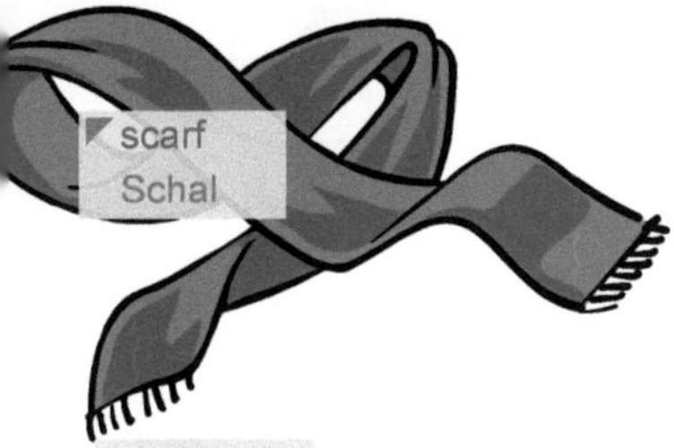

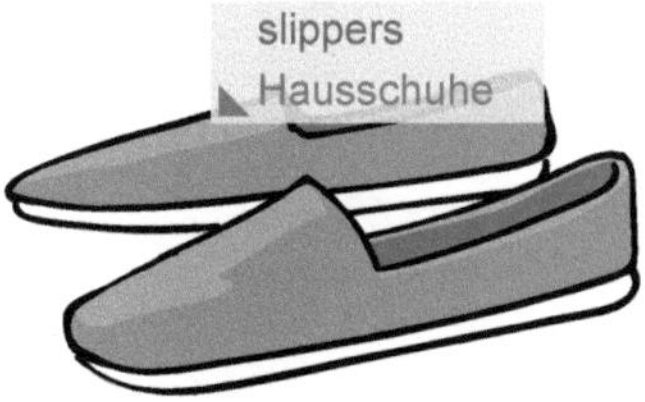

scarf
Schal

belt
Gürtel

umbrella
Regenschirm

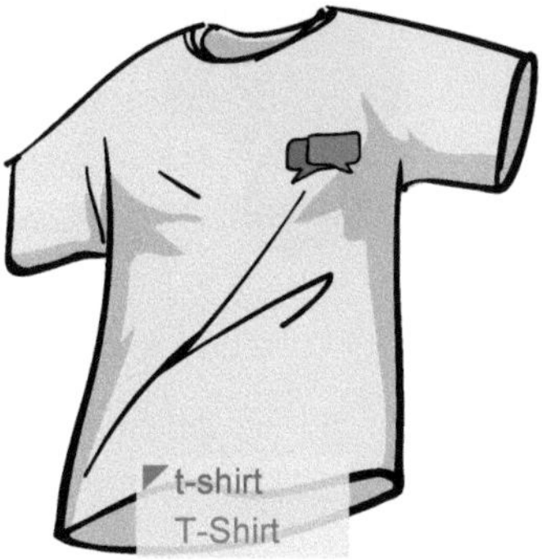

t-shirt
T-Shirt

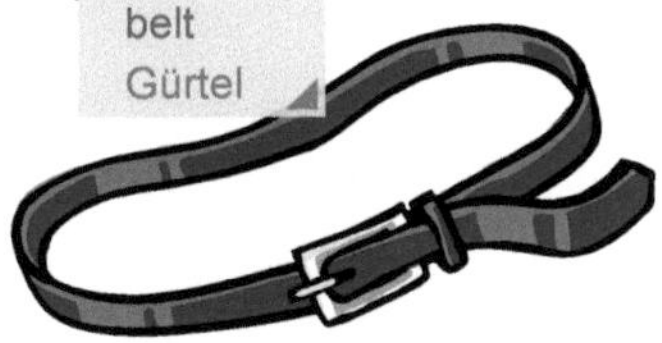

sneakers
Turnschuhe

boots
Stiefel

slippers
Hausschuhe

sandals

Sandalen

shoes

Schuhe

rubber boots

Gummistiefel

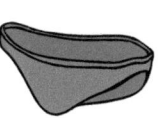

underwear

Unterhose

bra

Büstenhalter

undershirt

Unterhemd

clothing - Kleidung

body

Body

pants

Hose

jeans

Jeans

skirt

Rock

blouse

Bluse

shirt

Hemd

pullover

Pullover

sweater

Kapuzenpullover

blazer

Blazer

jacket

Jacke

coat

Mantel

raincoat

Regenmantel

costume

Kostüm

dress

Kleid

wedding dress

Hochzeitskleid

suit

Anzug

nightgown

Nachthemd

pajamas

Pyjama

sari

Sari

headscarf

Kopftuch

turban

Turban

burka

Burka

kaftan

Kaftan

abaya

Abaya

swimsuit

Badeanzug

trunks

Badehose

shorts

kurze Hose

tracksuit

Jogginganzug

apron

Schürze

gloves

Handschuhe

button

Knopf

glasses

Brille

bracelet

Armband

necklace

Halskette

ring

Ring

earring

Ohrring

cap

Mütze

coat hanger

Kleiderbügel

hat

Hut

tie

Krawatte

zip

Reißverschluss

helmet

Helm

braces

Hosenträger

school uniform

Schuluniform

uniform

Uniform

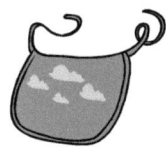

bib

Lätzchen

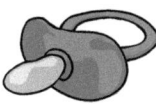

pacifier

Schnuller

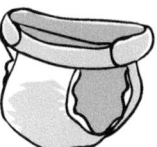

diaper

Windel

office
Büro

server
Server
filing cabinet
Aktenschrank
printer
Drucker
paper
Papier
monitor
Monitor
mouse
Maus
desk
Schreibtisch
folder
Ordner
keyboard
Tastatur
waste-paper basket
Papierkorb
computer
Computer
chair
Sessel

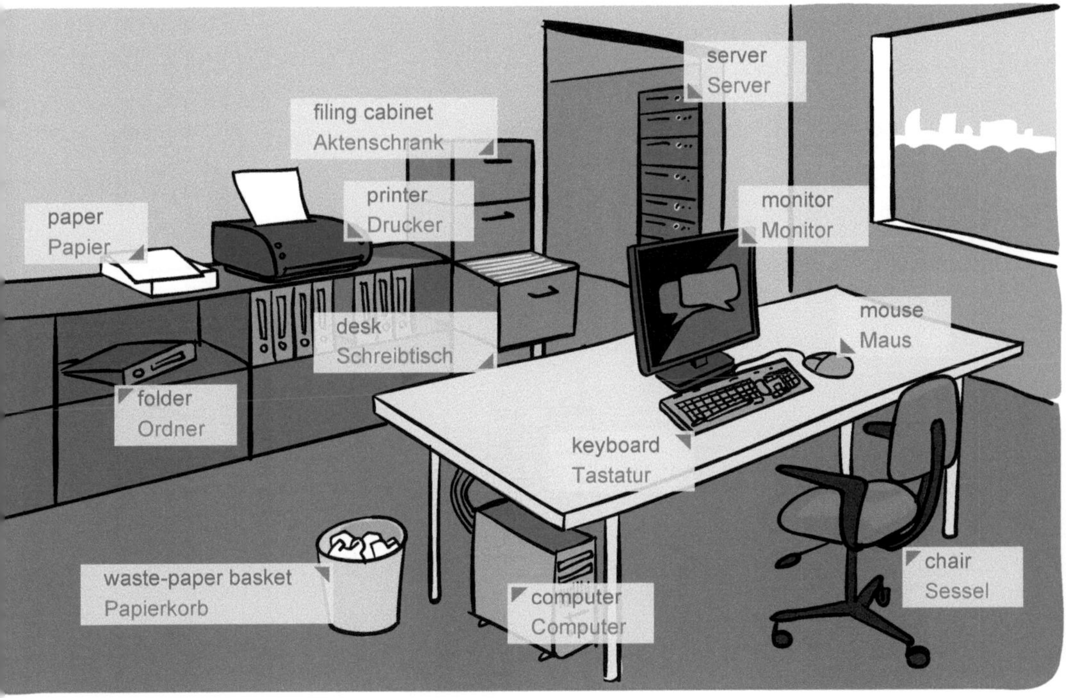

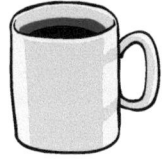

coffee mug

Kaffeebecher

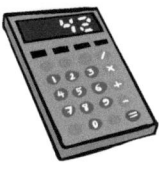

calculator

Taschenrechner

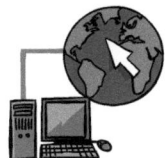

internet

Internet

laptop	letter	message
Laptop	Brief	Nachricht

cell phone	network	photocopier
Handy	Netzwerk	Kopierer

software	telephone	plug socket
Software	Telefon	Steckdose
	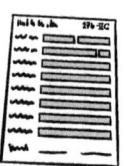	
fax machine	form	document
Fax	Formular	Dokument

buy

kaufen

pay

bezahlen

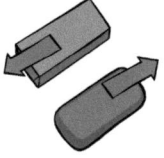

trade

handeln

money

Geld

dollar

Dollar

euro

Euro

yen

Yen

rouble

Rubel

Swiss franc

Franken

renminbi yuan

Renminbi Yuan

rupee

Rupie

cash point

Bankomat

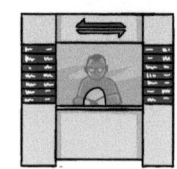

currency exchange office

Wechselstube

gold

Gold

silver

Silber

oil

Öl

energy

Energie

price

Preis

contract

Vertrag

tax

Steuer

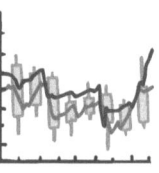

stock

Aktie

work

arbeiten

employee

Angestellte

employer

Arbeitgeber

factory

Fabrik

shop

Geschäft

economy - Wirtschaft

occupations
Berufe

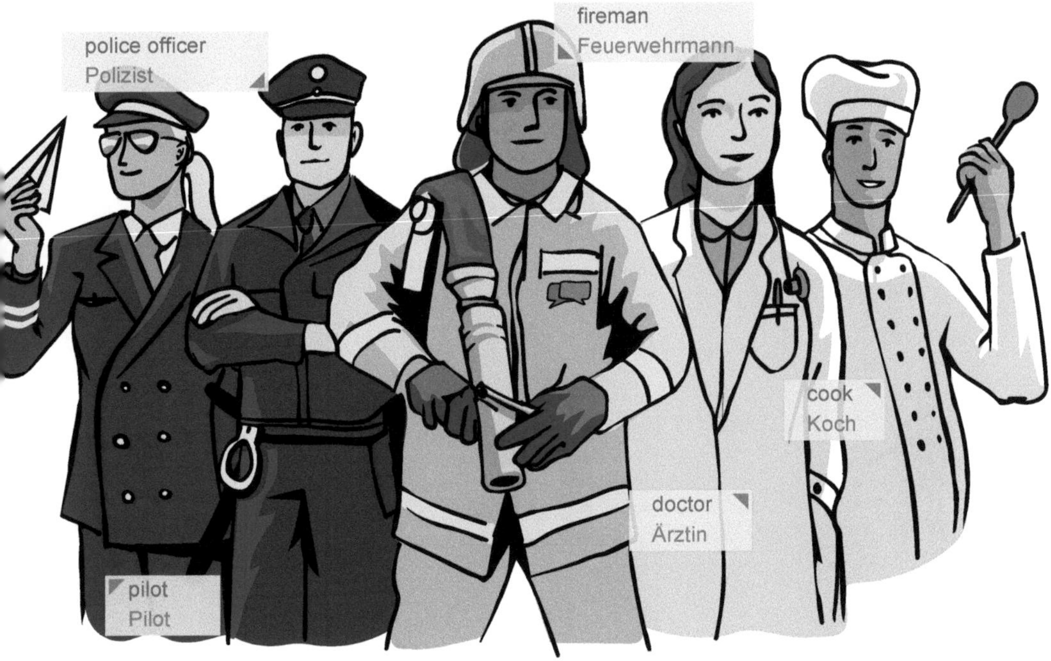

police officer
Polizist
fireman
Feuerwehrmann
cook
Koch
doctor
Ärztin
pilot
Pilot

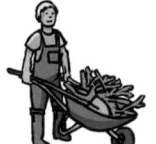

gardener
Gärtner

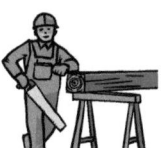

carpenter
Tischler

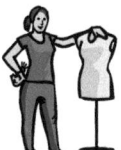

seamstress
Schneiderin

judge
Richter

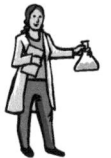

chemist
Chemikerin

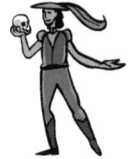

actor
Schauspieler

bus driver

Busfahrer

taxi driver

Taxifahrer

fisherman

Fischer

cleaning lady

Putzfrau

roofer

Dachdecker

waiter

Kellner

hunter

Jäger

painter

Maler

baker

Bäcker

electrician

Elektriker

builder

Bauarbeiter

engineer

Ingenieur

butcher

Schlachter

plumber

Installateur

postman

Briefträgerin

occupations - Berufe

soldier

Soldat

architect

Architekt

cashier

Kassiererin

florist

Blumenhändlerin

hairdresser

Friseur

conductor

Schaffner

mechanic

Mechaniker

captain

Kapitän

dentist

Zahnärztin

scientist

Wissenschaftler

rabbi

Rabbi

imam

Imam

monk

Mönch

pastor

Pfarrer

tools
Werkzeuge

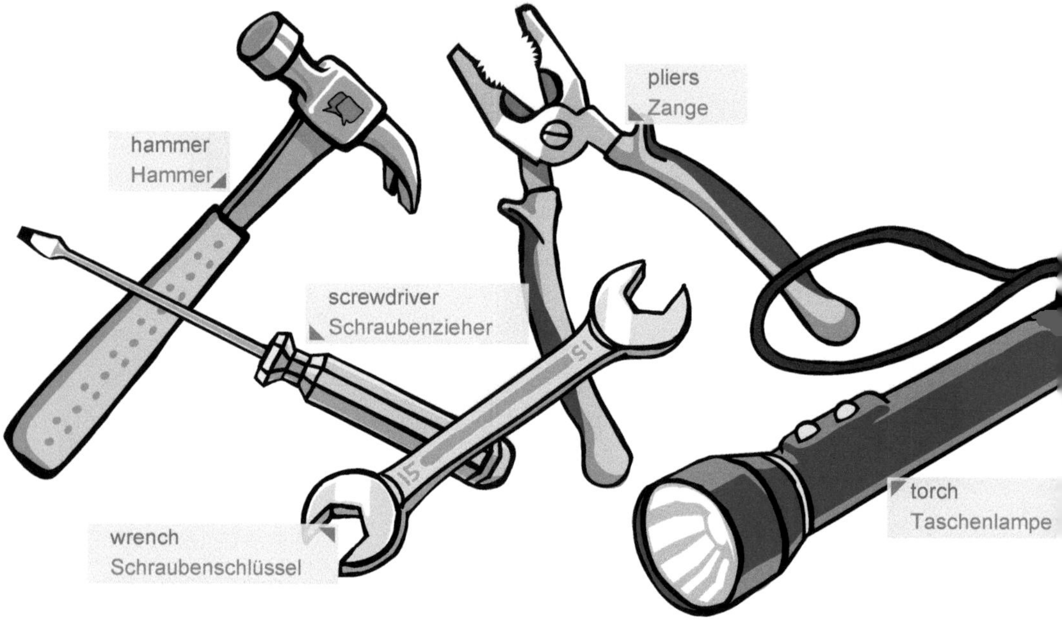

hammer
Hammer
pliers
Zange
screwdriver
Schraubenzieher
torch
Taschenlampe
wrench
Schraubenschlüssel

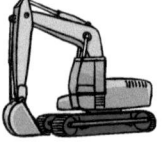

excavator

Bagger

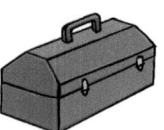

toolbox

Werkzeugkasten

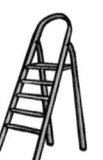

ladder

Leiter

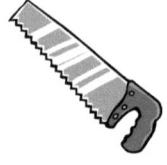

saw

Säge

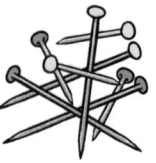

nails

Nägel

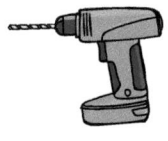

drill

Bohrer

repair

reparieren

shovel

Schaufel

Damn!

Scheiße!

dustpan

Kehrschaufel

paint can

Farbtopf

screws

Schrauben

musical instruments
Musikinstrumente

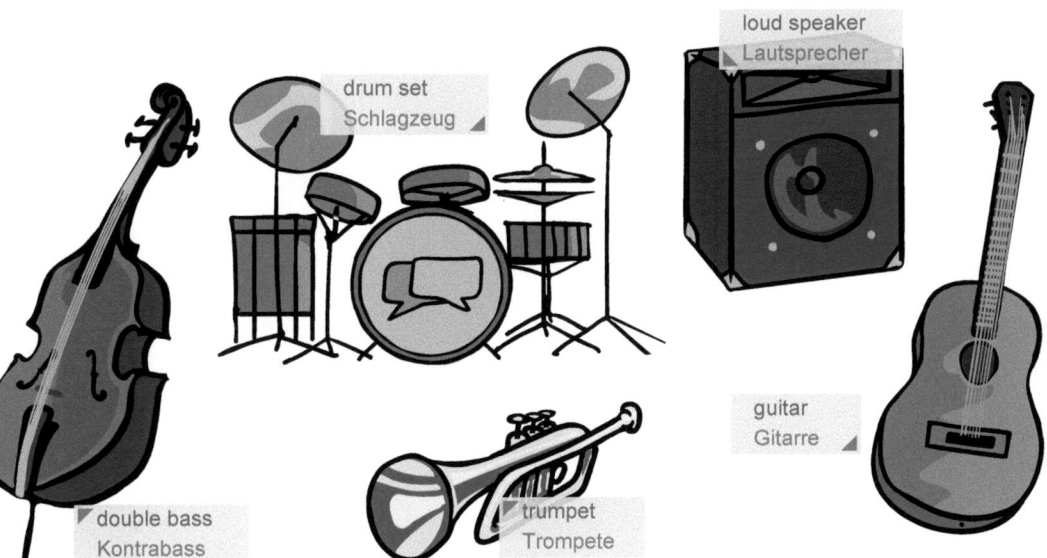

drum set
Schlagzeug

loud speaker
Lautsprecher

guitar
Gitarre

double bass
Kontrabass

trumpet
Trompete

piano

Klavier

violin

Violine

bass

Bass

timpani

Pauke

drums

Trommeln

keyboard

Tastatur

saxophone

Saxophon

flute

Flöte

microphone

Mikrofon

zoo

Zoo

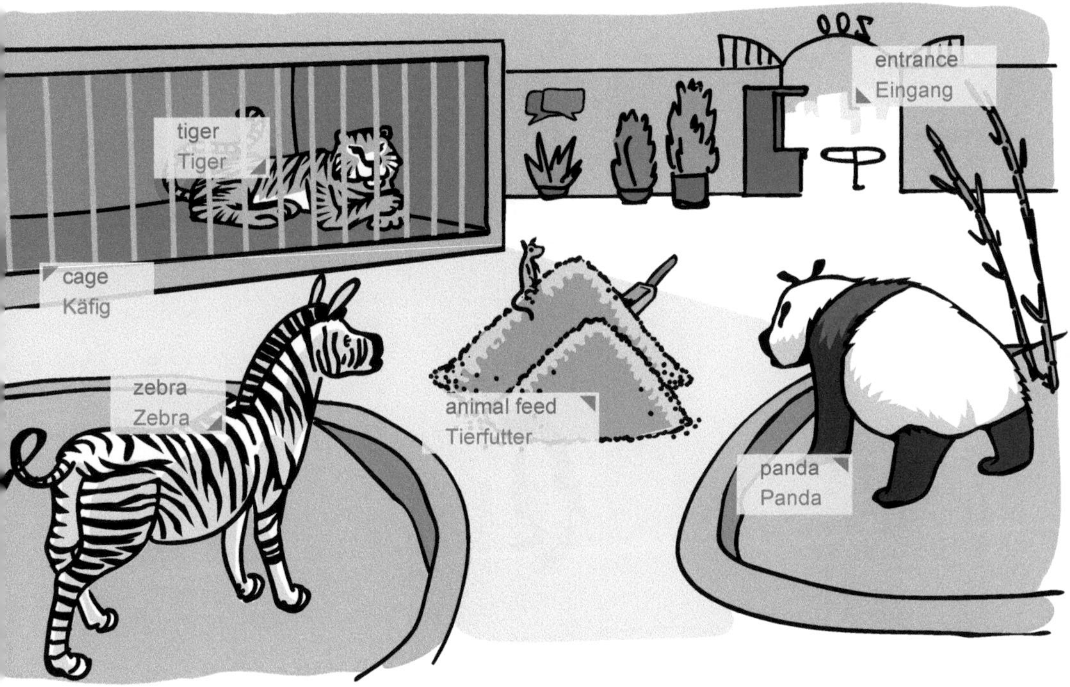

entrance
Eingang
tiger
Tiger
cage
Käfig
zebra
Zebra
animal feed
Tierfutter
panda
Panda

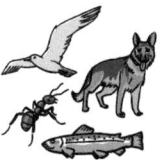

animals

Tiere

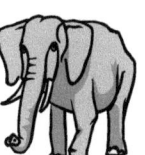

elephant

Elefant

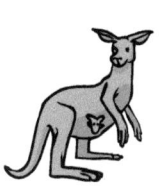

kangaroo

Känguru

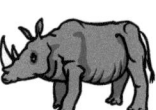

rhino

Nashorn

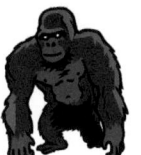

gorilla

Gorilla

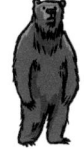

bear

Bär

camel

Kamel

ostrich

Strauß

lion

Löwe

monkey

Affe

flamingo

Flamingo

parrot

Papagei

polar bear

Eisbär

penguin

Pinguin

shark

Hai

peacock

Pfau

snake

Schlange

crocodile

Krokodil

zookeeper

Zoowärter

seal

Robbe

jaguar

Jaguar

zoo - Zoo

pony

Pony

leopard

Leopard

hippo

Nilpferd

giraffe

Giraffe

eagle

Adler

boar

Wildschwein

fish

Fisch

turtle

Schildkröte

walrus

Walross

fox

Fuchs

gazelle

Gazelle

American football
American Football

cycling
Radfahren

tennis
Tennis

basketball
Basketball

swimming
Schwimmen

boxing
Boxen

ice hockey
Eishockey

soccer
Fußball

badminton
Badminton

athletics
Leichtathletik

handball
Handball

skiing
Skifahren

polo
Polo

jump
springen

laugh
lachen

hug
umarmen

walk
gehen

sing
singen

dream
träumen

pray
beten

kiss
küssen

write
schreiben

draw
zeichnen

show
zeigen

push
drücken

give
geben

take
nehmen

have

haben

do

machen

be

sein

stand

stehen

run

laufen

pull

ziehen

throw

werfen

fall

fallen

lie

liegen

wait

warten

carry

tragen

sit

sitzen

get dressed

anziehen

sleep

schlafen

wake up

aufwachen

activities - Aktivitäten

look at

ansehen

cry

weinen

stroke

streicheln

comb

frisieren

talk

reden

understand

verstehen

ask

fragen

listen

hören

drink

trinken

eat

essen

tidy up

zusammenräumen

love

lieben

cook

kochen

drive

fahren

fly

fliegen

sail

segeln

calculate

rechnen

read

lesen

learn

lernen

work

arbeiten

marry

heiraten

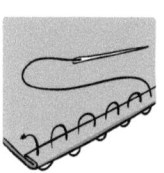

sew

nähen

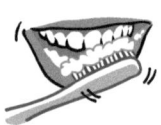

brush teeth

Zähne putzen

kill

töten

smoke

rauchen

send

senden

activities - Aktivitäten

family
Familie

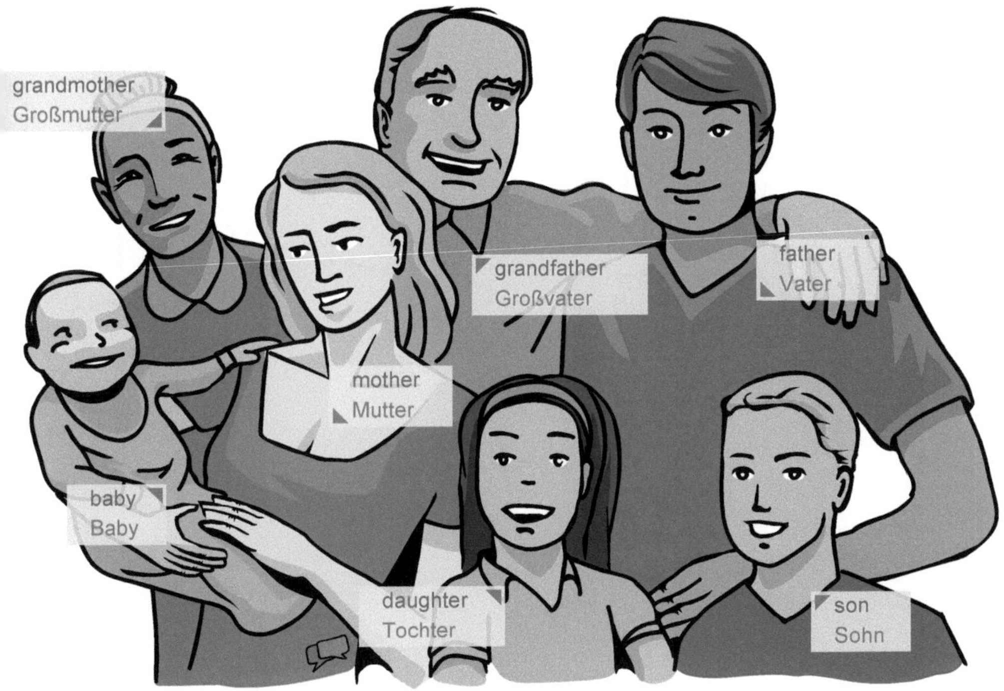
grandmother
Großmutter
grandfather
Großvater
father
Vater
mother
Mutter
baby
Baby
daughter
Tochter
son
Sohn

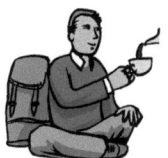

guest
Gast

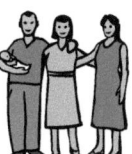

aunt
Tante

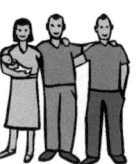

uncle
Onkel

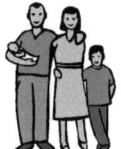

brother
Bruder

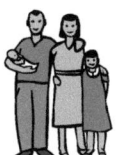

sister
Schwester

body

Körper

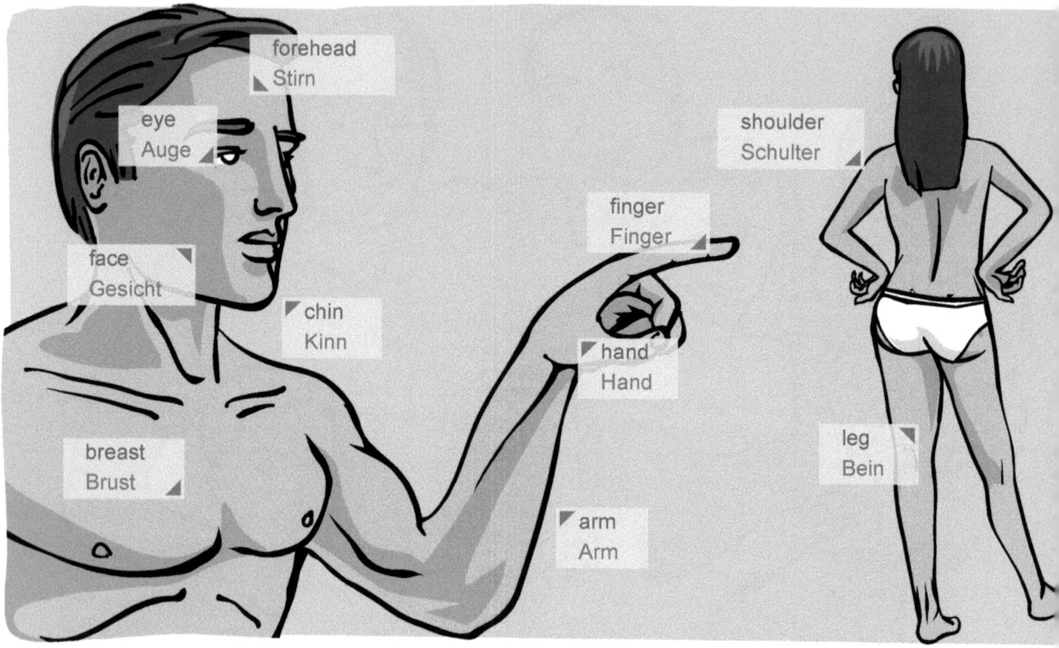

forehead
Stirn

eye
Auge

shoulder
Schulter

finger
Finger

face
Gesicht

chin
Kinn

hand
Hand

breast
Brust

leg
Bein

arm
Arm

baby
Baby

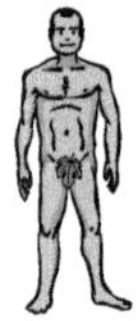

man
Mann

woman
Frau

girl
Mädchen

boy
Junge

head
Kopf

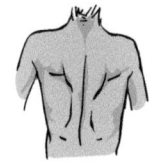

back

Rücken

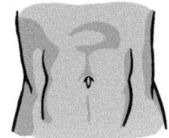

belly

Bauch

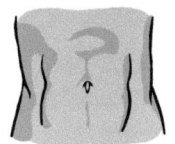

navel

Nabel

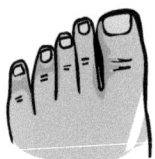

toe

Zeh

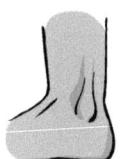

heel

Ferse

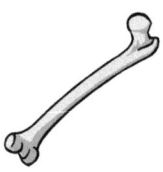

bone

Knochen

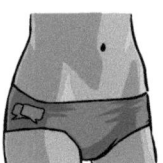

hip

Hüfte

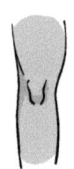

knee

Knie

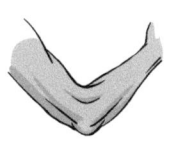

elbow

Ellbogen

nose

Nase

buttocks

Gesäß

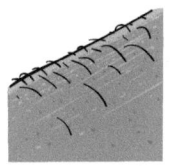

skin

Haut

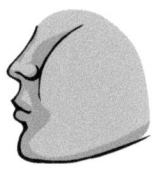

cheek

Wange

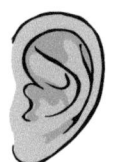

ear

Ohr

lip

Lippe

mouth

Mund

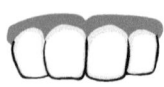

tooth

Zahn

tongue

Zunge

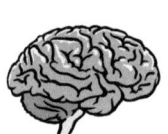

brain

Gehirn

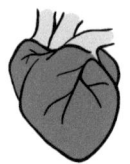

heart

Herz

muscle

Muskel

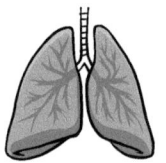

lung

Lunge

liver

Leber

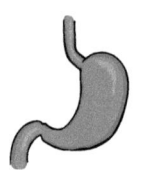

stomach

Magen

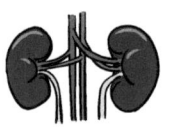

kidneys

Nieren

sex

Geschlechtsverkehr

condom

Kondom

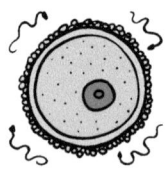

ovum

Eizelle

semen

Sperma

pregnancy

Schwangerschaft

body - Körper

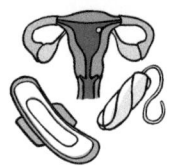

menstruation

Menstruation

vagina

Vagina

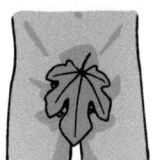

penis

Penis

eyebrow

Augenbraue

hair

Haar

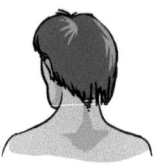

neck

Hals

hospital
Spital

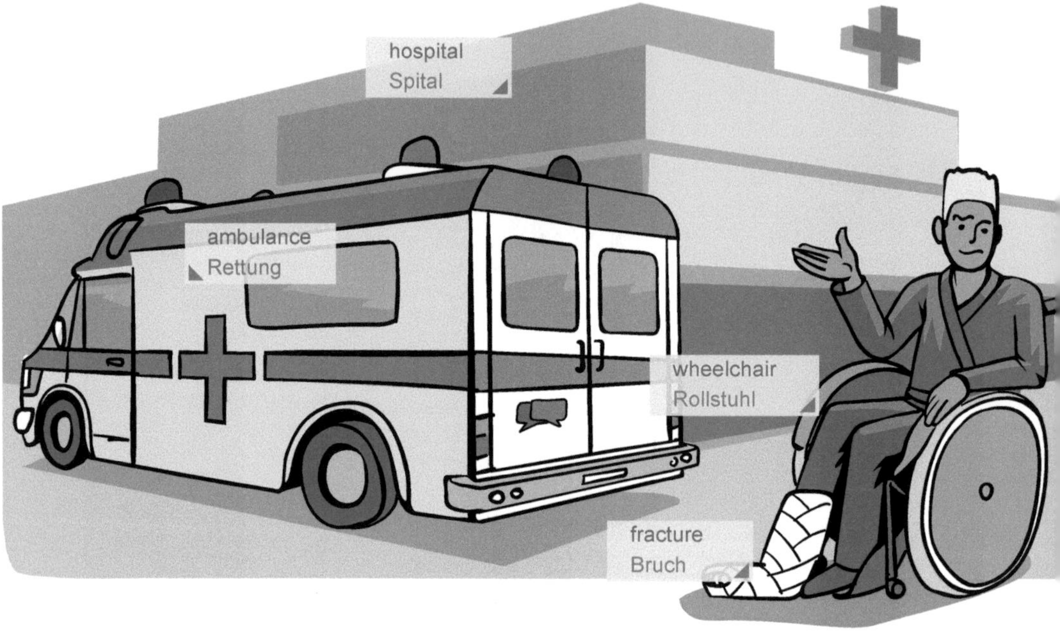

hospital
Spital
ambulance
Rettung
wheelchair
Rollstuhl
fracture
Bruch

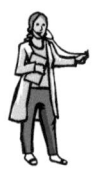

doctor
Ärztin

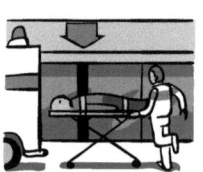

emergency room
Notaufnahme

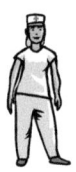

nurse
Krankenschwester

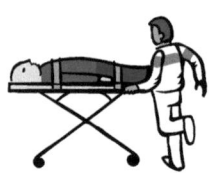

emergency
Notfall

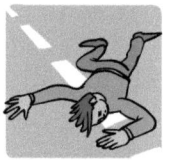

unconscious
ohnmächtig

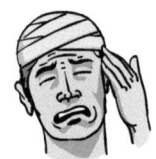

pain
Schmerz

injury

Verletzung

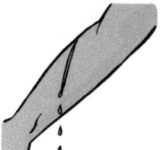

bleeding

Blutung

heart attack

Herzinfarkt

stroke

Schlaganfall

allergy

Allergie

cough

Husten

fever

Fieber

flu

Grippe

diarrhea

Durchfall

headache

Kopfschmerzen

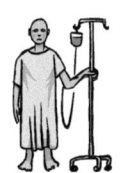

cancer

Krebs

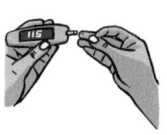

diabetes

Diabetes

surgeon

Chirurg

scalpel

Skalpell

operation

Operation

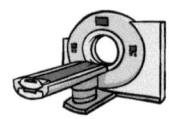

CT

CT

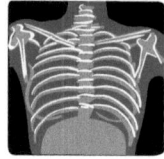

x-ray

Röntgen

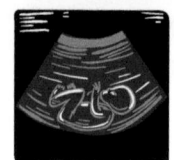

ultrasound

Ultraschall

face mask

Maske

disease

Krankheit

waiting room

Wartezimmer

crutch

Krücke

plaster

Pflaster

bandage

Verband

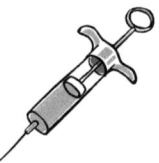

injection

Injektion

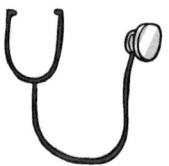

stethoscope

Stethoskop

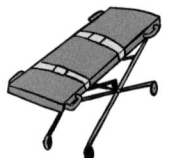

stretcher

Trage

clinical thermometer

Thermometer

birth

Geburt

overweight

Übergewicht

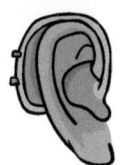

hearing aid

Hörgerät

disinfectant

Desinfektionsmittel

infection

Infektion

virus

Virus

HIV / AIDS

HIV / AIDS

medicine

Medizin

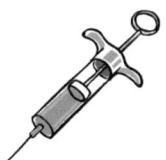

vaccination

Impfung

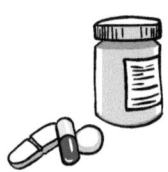

tablets

Tabletten

pill

Pille

emergency call

Notruf

blood pressure monitor

Blutdruckmesser

ill / healthy

krank / gesund

Help!

Hilfe!

alarm

Alarm

assault

Überfall

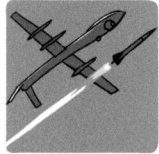

attack

Angriff

danger

Gefahr

emergency exit

Notausgang

Fire!

Feuer!

fire extinguisher

Feuerlöscher

accident

Unfall

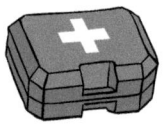

first-aid kit

Erste-Hilfe-Koffer

SOS

SOS

police

Polizei

Europe

Europa

North America

Nordamerika

South America

Südamerika

Africa

Afrika

Asia

Asien

Australia

Australien

Atlantic

Atlantik

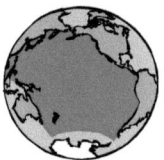

Pacific

Pazifik

Indian Ocean

Indische Ozean

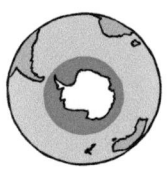

Antarctic Ocean

Antarktische Ozean

Arctic Ocean

Arktische Ozean

North pole

Nordpol

South pole

Südpol

Antarctica

Antarktis

earth

Erde

land

Land

sea

Meer

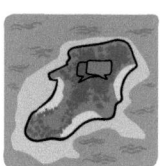

island

Insel

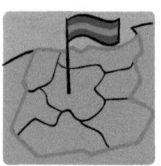

nation

Nation

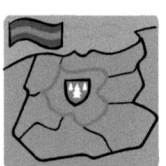

state

Staat

clock face

Ziffernblatt

hour hand

Stundenzeiger

minute hand

Minutenzeiger

second hand

Sekundenzeiger

What time is it?

Wie spät ist es?

day

Tag

time

Zeit

now

jetzt

digital watch

Digitaluhr

minute

Minute

hour

Stunde

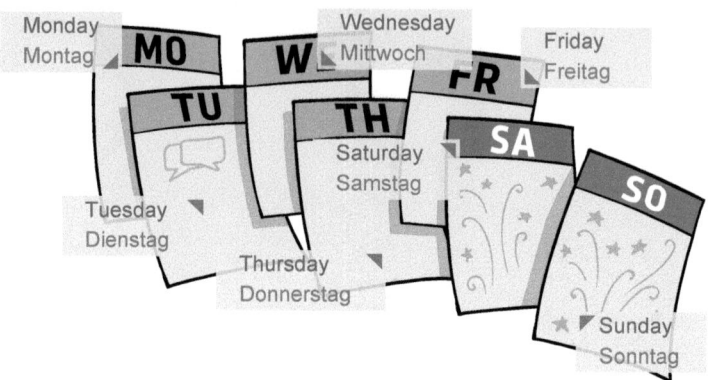

Monday / Montag — MO
Tuesday / Dienstag — TU
Wednesday / Mittwoch — W
Thursday / Donnerstag — TH
Friday / Freitag — FR
Saturday / Samstag — SA
Sunday / Sonntag — SO

yesterday

gestern

today

heute

tomorrow

morgen

morning

Morgen

noon

Mittag

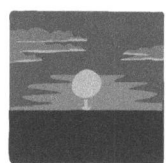

evening

Abend

workdays

Arbeitstage

weekend

Wochenende

year
Jahr

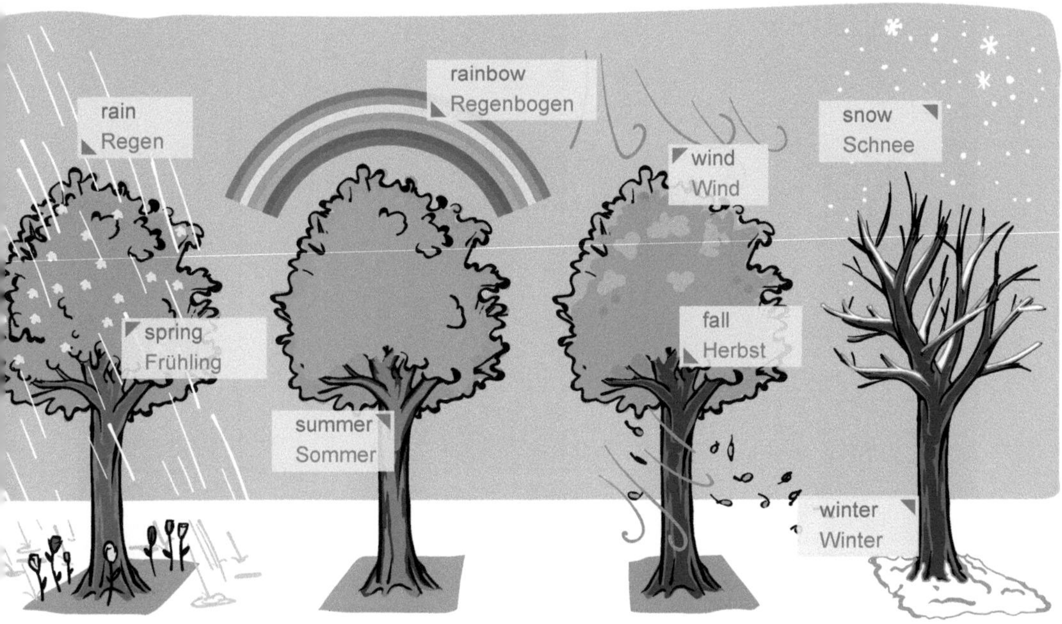

rain
Regen
rainbow
Regenbogen
wind
Wind
snow
Schnee
spring
Frühling
fall
Herbst
summer
Sommer
winter
Winter

4.APRIL	11°	
5.APRIL	4°	
6.APRIL	13°	
7.APRIL	8°	
8.APRIL	10°	

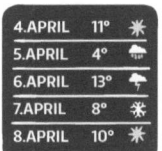

weather forecast

Wettervorhersage

F
C
120
90
60
30
0
-30
40
30
20
10
0
-10
-20

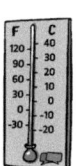

thermometer

Thermometer

sunshine

Sonnenschein

cloud

Wolke

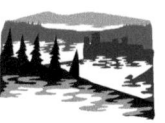

fog

Nebel

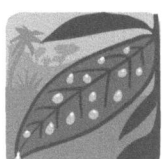

humidity

Luftfeuchtigkeit

lightning

Blitz

thunder

Donner

storm

Sturm

hail

Hagel

monsoon

Monsun

flood

Flut

ice

Eis

January

Jänner

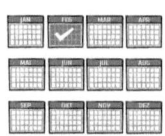

February

Februar

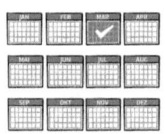

March

März

April

April

May

Mai

June

Juni

July

Juli

August

August

year - Jahr

September
September

October
Oktober

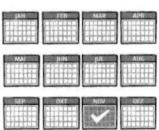

November
November

December
Dezember

shapes
Formen

circle
Kreis

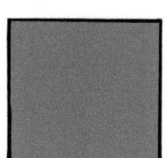

square
Quadrat

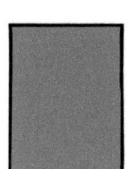

rectangle
Rechteck

triangle
Dreieck

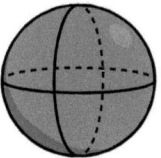

sphere
Kugel

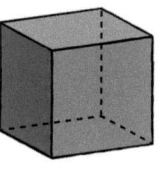

cube
Würfel

white

weiß

yellow

gelb

orange

orange

pink

pink

red

rot

purple

lila

blue

blau

green

grün

brown

braun

gray

grau

black

schwarz

a lot / a little

viel / wenig

angry / calm

wütend / friedlich

beautiful / ugly

hübsch / hässlich

beginning / end

Anfang / Ende

big / small

groß / klein

bright / dark

hell / dunkel

brother / sister

Bruder / Schwester

clean / dirty

sauber / schmutzig

complete / incomplete

vollständig / unvollständig

day / night

Tag / Nacht

dead / alive

tot / lebendig

wide / narrow

breit / schmal

edible / inedible

genießbar / ungenießbar

evil / kind

böse / freundlich

excited / bored

aufgeregt / gelangweilt

fat / thin

dick / dünn

first / last

zuerst / zuletzt

friend / enemy

Freund / Feind

full / empty

voll / leer

hard / soft

hart / weich

heavy / light

schwer / leicht

hunger / thirst

Hunger / Durst

ill / healthy

krank / gesund

illegal / legal

illegal / legal

intelligent / stupid

gescheit / dumm

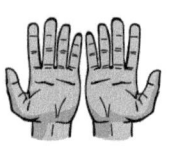

left / right

links / rechts

near / far

nah / fern

opposites - Gegenteile

new / used

neu / gebraucht

nothing / something

nichts / etwas

old / young

alt / jung

on / off

an / aus

open / closed

offen / geschlossen

quiet / loud

leise / laut

rich / poor

reich / arm

right / wrong

richtig / falsch

rough / smooth

rau / glatt

sad / happy

traurig / glücklich

short / long

kurz / lang

slow / fast

langsam / schnell

wet / dry

nass / trocken

warm / cool

warm / kühl

war / peace

Krieg / Frieden

0

zero

null

1

one

eins

2

two

zwei

3

three

drei

4

four

vier

5

five

fünf

6

six

sechs

7

seven

sieben

8

eight

acht

9

nine

neun

10

ten

zehn

11

eleven

elf

12
twelve
zwölf

13
thirteen
dreizehn

14
fourteen
vierzehn

15
fifteen
fünfzehn

16
sixteen
sechzehn

17
seventeen
siebzehn

18
eighteen
achtzehn

19
nineteen
neunzehn

20
twenty
zwanzig

100
hundred
hundert

1.000
thousand
tausend

1.000.000
million
Million

languages
Sprachen

English
....
Englisch

American English
....
Amerikanisches Englisch

Chinese Mandarin
....
Chinesisch (Mandarin)

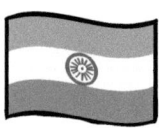

Hindi
....
Hindi

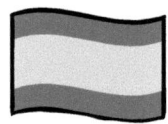

Spanish
....
Spanisch

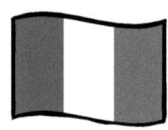

French
....
Französisch

Arabic
....
Arabisch

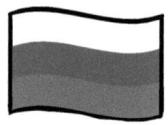

Russian
....
Russisch

Portuguese
....
Portugiesisch

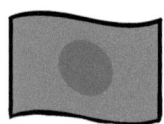

Bengali
....
Bengalisch

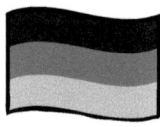

German
....
Deutsch

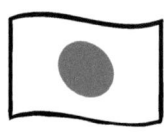

Japanese
....
Japanisch

I

ich

you

du

he / she / it

er / sie / es

we

wir

you

ihr

they

sie

who?

Wer?

what?

Was?

how?

Wie?

where?

Wo?

when?

Wann?

name

Name

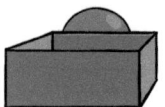

behind

hinter

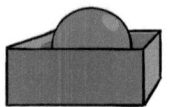

in

in

in front of

vor

over

über

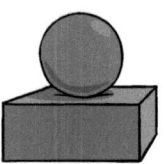

on

auf

under

unter

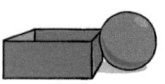

beside

neben

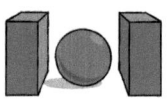

between

zwischen

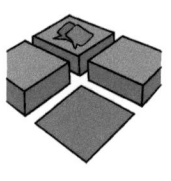

place

Ort